Securing Our Homeland

U.S. Department of Homeland Security Strategic Plan

 Homeland Security

In January 2003, the Department of Homeland Security became the Nation's 15th and newest Cabinet department, consolidating 22 previously disparate agencies under one unified organization. One year ago, no single federal department had homeland security as its primary objective. Now it is our mission. We are integrating our resources to meet a common goal. Our most important job is to protect the American people and our way of life from terrorism. We have a single, clear line of authority to get the job done. While we can never eliminate the potential for attack, particularly in a society that's as open, as diverse, and as large as ours, we will significantly reduce the Nation's vulnerability to terrorism and terrorist attack over time. Through partnerships with state, local and tribal governments and the private sector, we are working to ensure the highest level of protection and preparedness for the country and the citizens we serve.

This plan outlines our approach to implement the National Strategy to secure the United States from terrorist threats and attacks, and prepare our country by building up capacity to respond if either occurs. It provides the frame of reference in which we will set priorities and focus our operations. We, in the Department of Homeland Security, are working to protect our fellow citizens and our very way of life by securing our borders, our airports, our waterways and our critical infrastructure. We are increasing our nation's ability to respond to emergencies. We are protecting the rights of American citizens and enhancing public services. We understand our mission. The task before us is difficult, but not impossible. We undertake the challenges before us with the understanding that Americans do not live in fear. We live in freedom, and we will never let that freedom go.

Securing Our Homeland

U. S. Department of Homeland Security Strategic Plan

2004

Contents

3 Introduction

4 Vision and Mission

5 Core Values

6 Guiding Principles

9 Summary

10 Goals and Objectives

46 Organizational Chart

47 A Day in the Life

52 Key Factors

54 Implementation

55 Evaluation

56 Communication

Securing Our Homeland

Vision, Mission, Core Values & Guiding Principles

Introduction

The attack on our homeland of September 11, 2001, was an assault on the ideals that make our nation great. We were reminded that the values we hold dear must not be taken for granted. From these tragic events, a stronger union has emerged. Our citizens, and those of countries around the world, renewed their commitment to this nation and to the values for which it stands. In January of 2003, the United States Government established the Department of Homeland Security to focus America's efforts to thwart those who seek to do us harm. The Department has an overriding and urgent mission: secure the American homeland and protect the American people.

The President's *National Strategy for Homeland Security* outlined the basic purpose behind establishing the Department and provided an overview of its homeland security responsibilities. The Department's Strategic Plan interprets the *National Strategy for Homeland Security* and prescribes the vision for our workforce, our stakeholders and the American people. The Department's strategic goals and objectives are directly linked to accomplishing the three objectives of the National Strategy:

1) Prevent terrorist attacks within the United States;
2) Reduce America's vulnerability to terrorism; and
3) Minimize the damage and recover from attacks that do occur.

The Department's Strategic Plan governs the development of strategies, programs and projects, and ultimately is reflected in the Department's budget. Our plan reflects the determination of our nation to prevail against terror, to protect our homeland and to create a better world in the process. Describing who we are and what we do, it conveys the beliefs and values that govern our conduct. It outlines what we will accomplish. This document provides the vision and direction, as well as the goals and objectives for the Department while our detailed budget plan describes how we will achieve results. Each program in the budget plan will be linked to our goals and objectives and will have timelines and ownership associated with specific performance.

This is our action plan for securing our homeland. The Department of Homeland Security was created not to increase the size of the government, but to focus and integrate our collective efforts. Employees of this new organization come to work every day knowing their most important job is to protect their fellow citizens. We are stronger and better prepared today than we were in the past, and in the future will be stronger still. We have learned a great deal since September 11, 2001, and will act on every lesson to ensure the security of the American people.

Vision

Preserving our freedoms, protecting America.... we secure our homeland.

Mission

We will lead the unified national effort to secure America. We will prevent and deter terrorist attacks and protect against and respond to threats and hazards to the Nation. We will ensure safe and secure borders, welcome lawful immigrants and visitors, and promote the free-flow of commerce.

Core Values

Personal attributes expected of every Department of Homeland Security employee.

Integrity. **"Service before Self"**
Each of us serves something far greater than ourselves. To our nation, we represent the President and the Congress. To the world, seeking to visit or do business with us, we are often the first Americans they meet. We will faithfully execute the duties and responsibilities entrusted to us, and we will maintain the highest ethical and professional standards.

Vigilance. **"Guarding America"**
We will relentlessly identify and deter threats that pose a danger to the safety of the American people. As a Department, we will be constantly on guard against threats, hazards, or dangers that threaten our values and our way of life.

Respect. **"Honoring our Partners"**
We will value highly the relationships we build with our customers, partners and stakeholders. We will honor concepts such as liberty and democracy, for which America stands.

Guiding Principles

The philosophy that informs and shapes decision making and provides normative criteria that governs the actions of policy makers and employees in performing their work.

Protect Civil Rights and Civil Liberties.
We will defend America while protecting the freedoms that define America. Our strategies and actions will be consistent with the individual rights and liberties enshrined by our Constitution and the Rule of Law. While we seek to improve the way we collect and share information about terrorists, we will nevertheless be vigilant in respecting the confidentiality and protecting the privacy of our citizens. We are committed to securing our nation while protecting civil rights and civil liberties.

Integrate Our Actions.
We will blend 22 previously disparate agencies, each with its employees, mission and culture, into a single, unified Department whose mission is to secure the homeland. The Department of Homeland Security will be a cohesive, capable and service-oriented organization whose cross-cutting functions will be optimized so that we may protect our nation against threats and effectively respond to disasters.

Build Coalitions and Partnerships.
Building new bridges to one another are as important as building new barriers against terrorism. We will collaborate and coordinate across traditional boundaries, both horizontally (between agencies) and vertically (among different levels of government). We will engage partners and stakeholders from federal, state, local, tribal and international governments, as well as the private sector and academia. We will work together to identify needs, provide service, share information and promote best practices. We will foster inter-connected systems, rooted in the precepts of federalism that reinforce rather than duplicate individual efforts. Homeland security is a national effort, not solely a federal one.

Develop Human Capital.

Our most valuable asset is not new equipment or technology, but rather our dedicated and patriotic employees. Their contributions will be recognized and valued by this Department. We will hire, train and place the very best people in jobs to which they are best suited. We are committed to personal and professional growth and will create new opportunities to train and to learn. We will create a model human resources management system that supports equally the mission of the Department and the people charged with achieving it.

Innovate.

We will introduce and apply new concepts and creative approaches that will help us meet the challenges of the present and anticipate the needs of the future. We will support innovation and agility within the public and private sector, both by providing resources and removing red tape so that new solutions reach the Department and the marketplace as soon as possible. We will harness our nation's best minds in science, medicine and technology to develop applications for homeland security. Above all, we will look for ways to constantly improve—we will recognize complacency as an enemy.

Be Accountable.

We will seek measurable progress as we identify vulnerabilities, detect evolving threats to the American homeland and prioritize our homeland security resources. We will assess our work, evaluate the results and incorporate lessons learned to enhance our performance. We will reward excellence and fix what we find to be broken. We will communicate our progress to the American people, operating as transparently as possible and routinely measuring the success of our progress.

Securing Our Homeland

Goals and Objectives

Summary

The *National Strategy for Homeland Security* and the *Homeland Security Act of 2002* served to mobilize and organize our nation to secure the homeland from terrorist attacks. This is an exceedingly complex mission that requires coordinated and focused effort from our entire society. To this end, the Department of Homeland Security was established to provide the unifying core of the vast national network of organizations and institutions involved in efforts to secure our homeland. Our first priority is to prevent further terrorist attacks within the United States. To reduce vulnerability without diminishing economic security, we gather intelligence and analyze threats, guard our nation's borders and airports, protect our critical infrastructure and coordinate response to the American people during times of disaster. The goals guide the full breadth of our activities (both terrorism and non-terrorism related):

1 **Awareness:** Identify and understand threats, assess vulnerabilities, determine potential impacts and disseminate timely information to our homeland security partners and the American public.

2 **Prevention:** Detect, deter and mitigate threats to our homeland.

3 **Protection:** Safeguard our people and their freedoms, critical infrastructure, property and the economy of our nation from acts of terrorism, natural disasters, or other emergencies.

4 **Response:** Lead, manage and coordinate the national response to acts of terrorism, natural disasters, or other emergencies.

5 **Recovery:** Lead national, state, local and private sector efforts to restore services and rebuild communities after acts of terrorism, natural disasters, or other emergencies.

6 **Service:** Serve the public effectively by facilitating lawful trade, travel and immigration.

7 **Organizational Excellence:** Value our most important resource, our people. Create a culture that promotes a common identity, innovation, mutual respect, accountability and teamwork to achieve efficiencies, effectiveness and operational synergies.

Awareness

Strategic Goal 1

Identify and understand threats, assess vulnerabilities, determine potential impacts and disseminate timely information to our homeland security partners and the American public.

Objective 1.1

Gather and fuse all terrorism related intelligence; analyze, and coordinate access to information related to potential terrorist or other threats.

Intelligence and information analysis is an integral component of our nation's overall efforts to protect against and reduce our vulnerability to terrorism. We will receive, assess and analyze information from law enforcement, the intelligence community and non-traditional sources (e.g., state and local, private sector) to increase situational awareness of terrorist threats and specific incidents. We will review and, as necessary, work to improve policies for law enforcement and intelligence information sharing within the Federal Government and between state and local authorities. Data collection and analysis capabilities will be supported through investment in, and development of, leading-edge information analysis, data mining, data warehousing and threat/vulnerability mapping applications and tools, and recruiting, training and retaining human analysts.

Objective 1.2

Identify and assess the vulnerability of critical infrastructure and key assets.

We will conduct and sustain a complete, current and accurate assessment of our nation's infrastructure sectors and assets. We will use modeling, simulation and risk-based analytic tools to prioritize our work with an emphasis on critical infrastructure and key resources that could be catastrophically exploited. By establishing this understanding of the full array of critical infrastructure facilities and assets, how they interact and the interdependencies across infrastructure sectors, we will be in a position to anticipate the national security, economic and public safety implications of terrorist attacks and will prioritize protective measures accordingly.

Objective 1.3

Develop timely, actionable and valuable information based on intelligence analysis and vulnerability assessments.

We will integrate intelligence, threat and infrastructure vulnerability information to provide our national leaders, decision makers and the owners and operators of our critical infrastructure and key assets with the increasingly targeted and actionable information necessary in the post 9/11 threat environment. We will build an intelligence analysis structure that coordinates with the rest of the Federal Government; as well as state, local and tribal governments; the private sector; and our international partners. Our national imperative is to improve the sharing, analysis, integration of all-source threat, risk and infrastructure vulnerability information so appropriate preventative and protective actions can be taken.

Objective 1.4

Ensure quick and accurate dissemination of relevant intelligence information to homeland security partners, including the public.

Securing the homeland is a joint effort of the Federal Government; state, local and tribal governments; the private sector; our international partners; and the public. Therefore we will work to empower those partners by disseminating relevant intelligence and threat information to them accurately and as quickly as possible. We will work with our partners to remove roadblocks to information sharing. We will administer the Homeland Security Advisory System, including the issuance of public advisories and coordination of warning information with other agencies. We will deploy and operate tools and secure communications channels to analyze and disseminate information to relevant agencies as quickly and efficiently as possible.

Prevention

Strategic Goal 2

Detect, deter and mitigate threats to our homeland.

Objective 2.1

Secure our borders against terrorists, means of terrorism, illegal drugs and other illegal activity.

We interdict terrorist activities by targeting unlawful migration of people, cargo, drugs and other contraband, while facilitating legitimate migration and commerce. The Department will enforce border security in an integrated fashion at ports of entry, on the borders, on the seas and before potential threats can reach our borders. Through the continued deployment of the appropriate balance of personnel, equipment and technology we will create "smart borders." Not only will we create more secure United States borders but, in conjunction with international partners, we will extend our zones of security beyond our physical borders identifying, prioritizing and interdicting threats to our nation before they arrive. We will develop and provide resources for a cohesive, unified enforcement capability that makes our border security effective, smarter and stronger.

Objective 2.2

Enforce trade and immigration laws.

We will enforce all applicable laws in an integrated fashion while facilitating free commerce and the flow of legal immigration and travel into the United States. We will interdict smuggling and stop other illegal activities that benefit terrorists and their supporters. We will build a unified, cohesive enforcement capability to actively conduct and co-ordinate law enforcement operations.

Objective 2.3

Provide operational end users with the technology and capabilities to detect and prevent terrorist attacks, means of terrorism and other illegal activities.

The Nation's technical superiority in science and technology is key to securing the homeland. We will use, leverage and enhance the vast resources and expertise of the Federal Government, private sector, academic community, non-governmental organizations and other scientific bodies. We will develop new capabilities to facilitate the sharing of information and analysis; test and assess threats and vulnerabilities; counter various threats, including weapons of mass destruction and illegal drugs; and mitigate the effects of terrorist attacks. We will also focus our efforts on developing technology to detect and prevent the illicit transport of chemical, biological, radiological and nuclear materials. We will develop and deploy the capabilities, equipment and systems needed to anticipate, respond to and recover from attacks on the homeland.

Objective 2.4

Ensure national and international policy, law enforcement and other actions to prepare for and prevent terrorism are coordinated.

We will effectively coordinate and communicate with other federal agencies; and, state, local and tribal governments; the private sector; and the American people. Increasing and coordinating information sharing between law enforcement, intelligence and military organizations will improve our ability to counter terrorists everywhere. We will coordinate training and education across multiple levels, both national and international, ensuring common standards and approaches to recognizing key indicators of future terrorist actions.

Objective 2.5

Strengthen the security of the Nation's transportation systems.

Transportation systems have the unique ability to be either a means of delivering weapons of terror or the target of a direct terrorist attack. Our domestic transportation system is intertwined inextricably with the global transportation infrastructure. Safety and security are two sides of the same coin. We will strengthen the security of the transportation network while we work to remove all threats or barriers to the safe movement of commerce and people. We will coordinate with federal, state, local and tribal agencies, as well as our international and private sector partners, to ensure the transportation system remains a safe and vital economic link, while preventing terrorists from using transportation conveyances or systems to deliver implements of destruction.

Objective 2.6

Ensure the security and integrity of the immigration system.

We will ensure that immigrants and non-immigrants comply with laws and security mandates to prevent persons who seek to exploit the economic and social benefits of immigration or engage in illegal activities from obtaining lawful status. We will strengthen legal protections and design programs appropriately to create a more secure immigration system. We make decisions in a timely and efficient manner by applying technology and allocating our resources to provide actionable and accurate information. We will ensure that those persons entitled to benefits receive them through verification services and encouraging employers to verify status. We will refer illegal aliens to enforcement entities for prosecution or removal from the United States.

Protection

Strategic Goal 3

Safeguard our people and their freedoms, critical infrastructure, property and the economy of our nation from acts of terrorism, natural disasters, or other emergencies.

Objective 3.1

Protect the public from acts of terrorism and other illegal activities.

We must not let the threat of terrorism alter the American way of life. We will identify and disrupt terrorist and criminals before they threaten the well being of American citizens. Our investigative efforts will focus on identifying the tools and conveyances used by terrorists and criminals, and apprehending suspect individuals. Through our partnerships with other agencies and through our own efforts we will coordinate and apply knowledge and skills acquired through years of practical use in drug interdiction and airspace security to remain at the forefront of global law enforcement and counter-terrorism efforts. We will ensure that our nation's shipping routes do not become avenues of entry for terrorists, their weapons, or supplies. We will conduct national and international investigations to gather evidence of violations of United States laws, and prevent terrorist groups from obtaining sensitive weapons of United States origin.

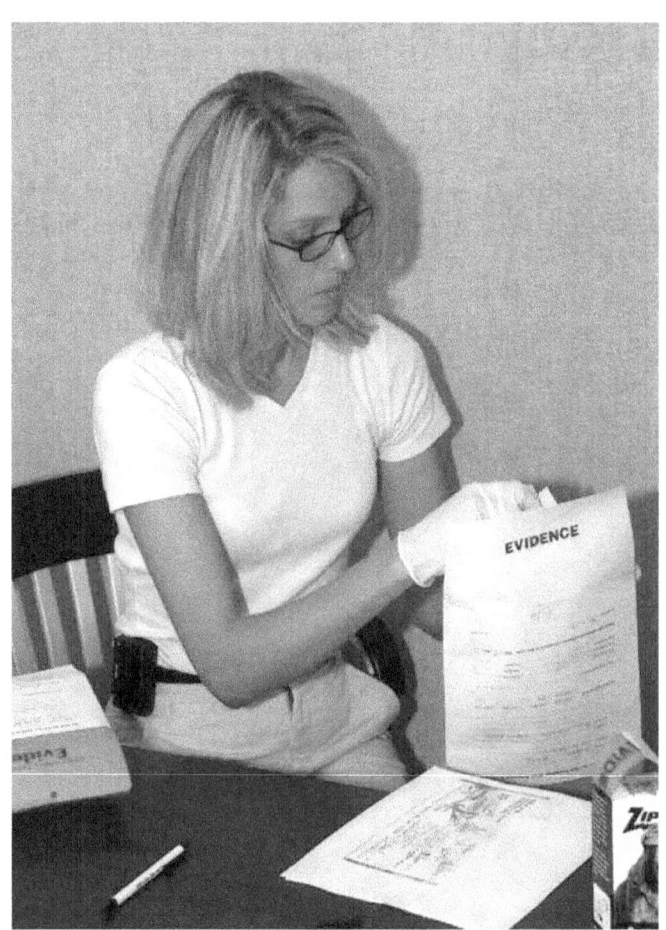

Objective 3.2

Reduce infrastructure vulnerability from acts of terrorism.

We will lead and coordinate a national effort to secure America's critical infrastructure. Protecting America's critical infrastructure is the shared responsibility of federal, state, local and tribal governments, in active partnership with the private sector, which owns approximately 85 percent of our nation's critical infrastructure. Using the results of modeling, simulation and analytic tools to prioritize our efforts, we will implement standardized and tiered protective measures that are rapidly adjustable to counter various levels of threat. We will coordinate the implementation of a comprehensive integrated national plan to protect both our physical and cyber infrastructure and significantly reduce vulnerabilities, while ensuring that government at all levels enables, and does not inhibit, the private sector's ability to carry out its protection responsibilities.

Objective 3.3

Protect against financial and electronic crimes, counterfeit currency, illegal bulk currency movement and identity theft.

A principal component of homeland security is economic security, including protection of the Nation's currency and financial payment systems. The Department of Homeland Security participates in task forces and other joint operations with the financial community and with federal, state, local and tribal law enforcement partners to investigate crimes targeting the stability, reliability and security of financial systems. To prevent, detect and investigate various forms of electronic crimes, we will operate a nationwide network of Electronic Crimes Task Forces. We will maintain an overseas investigative presence where criminal groups engage in the counterfeiting of United States currency and other financial crimes targeting our homeland. International drug traffickers steal $20 to $30 billion annually from the United States economy. Much of these illegal funds are shipped out of the United States as bulk currency. This weakens our economy and strengthens the ability of the international drug traffickers to destabilize the governments of their countries by bribery or to finance terrorist activities. We will investigate, identify and seize outbound shipments to take away this ability to fund illegal activities.

Objective 3.4

Secure the physical safety of the President, Vice President, visiting world leaders and other protectees.

We will protect our nation's leaders and visiting dignitaries from all threats, including terrorists and other criminals; natural, technological and man-made emergencies; and preventable accidents. We will coordinate with military, federal, state, local and tribal law enforcement organizations to ensure their safety. We will evaluate information received from law enforcement and intelligence agencies and other sources to investigate, apprehend and prosecute, if appropriate, those who pose a threat. We will ensure that protectees have a safe environment in which to continue their operations in the event of any threat contingency.

Objective 3.5

Ensure the continuity of government operations and essential functions in the event of crisis or disaster.

We will partner with other federal departments and agencies to ensure the continuous operation of the Federal Government and to secure the survival of an enduring constitutional government in times of attack, national emergency, or disaster. We will provide alternative facilities, equipment and communications capabilities to ensure that the Federal Government is capable of performing its essential functions, and that the Nation will continue to be governed as set forth in the United States Constitution.

Objective 3.6

Protect the marine environment and living marine resources.

We will partner with other nations; federal agencies; state, local and tribal governments; and responsible sectors of the maritime industry, to ensure the quality of our marine resources are protected. We will encourage, pursue and enforce bilateral and regional agreements with other governments to ensure that the world's living marine resources are properly maintained and managed. The ability to use unpolluted waters for transportation and recreation is vital to the safety of our citizens and the economy of our nation; we will work to ensure compliance with existing regulations and consider others that may be required to protect our marine environment. We will maintain an uncompromising commitment to the stewardship of our national living marine resources through the highest caliber enforcement of fisheries laws and regulations supporting the national policy.

Objective 3.7

Strengthen nationwide preparedness and mitigation against acts of terrorism, natural disasters, or other emergencies.

The best way to protect against the effects of harmful incidents is to be prepared. Preparedness and mitigation are important elements in reducing the impacts of acts of terror and other disasters. We will ensure all levels of public safety and emergency management are capable of rapid and effective response by establishing a unified, capabilities-based preparedness strategy incorporating all-hazards assessments, training, exercises and assistance for federal, state, tribal and local governments, first responders and communities. We will establish, implement and evaluate capabilities through a system of national standards, mutual aid systems and credentialing protocols, and supply technologies for rapid and interoperable communications, personal protection and incident management. We will implement and sustain a national citizen preparedness movement that includes private sector involvement. We will expand the Nation's community risk management capabilities and reduce the Nation's vulnerability to acts of terrorism and other disasters through effective vulnerability assessments and risk management programs.

Every day Homeland Security works to deliver on our
mission to better prevent, prepare and respond to a
terrorist attack. We pursued that mission not merely
by setting up one authority for 22 different agencies,
but by setting goals and meeting them, and we are,
and we will.

- Secretary Tom Ridge,

Remarks to the American Enterprise Institute
September 2, 2003

Response

Strategic Goal 4

Lead, manage and coordinate the national response to acts of terrorism, natural disasters, or other emergencies.

Objective 4.1

Reduce the loss of life and property by strengthening nationwide response readiness.

The Nation must have a vigorous capability to respond when disaster strikes. We will strengthen the national capability to respond to disasters of all types, including terrorism, through the integration of Department of Homeland Security response systems and teams and the completion of catastrophic all-hazard plans for the Nation's most vulnerable communities and geographic areas, including tactical elements to ensure coordinated response operations, logistics and support. We will provide health and medical response readiness through integrated planning, surge capacity to address health and medical emergencies or acts of terrorism and will develop the logistical capacity to provide intermediate emergency housing to large displaced populations following major disasters.

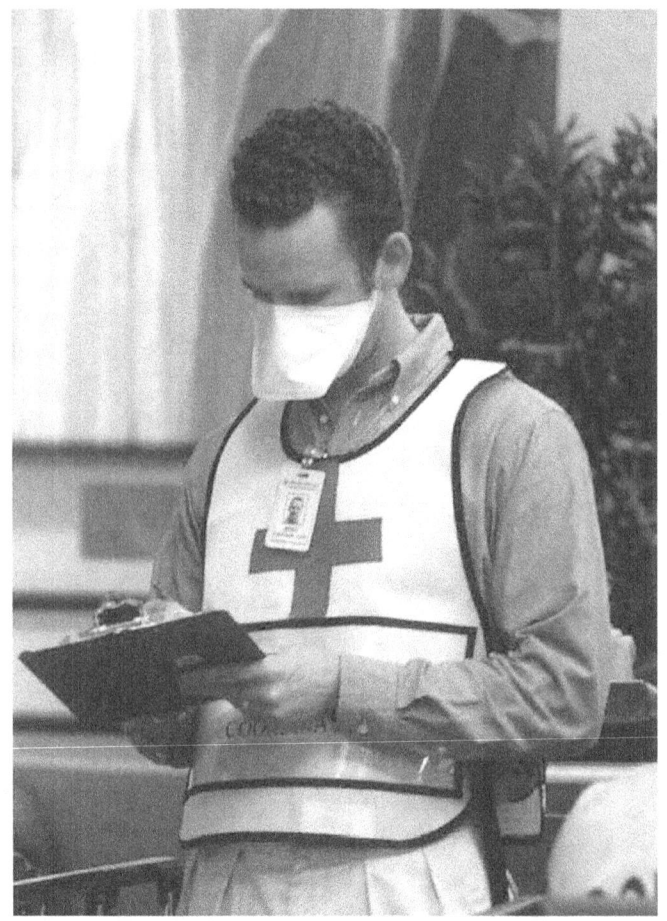

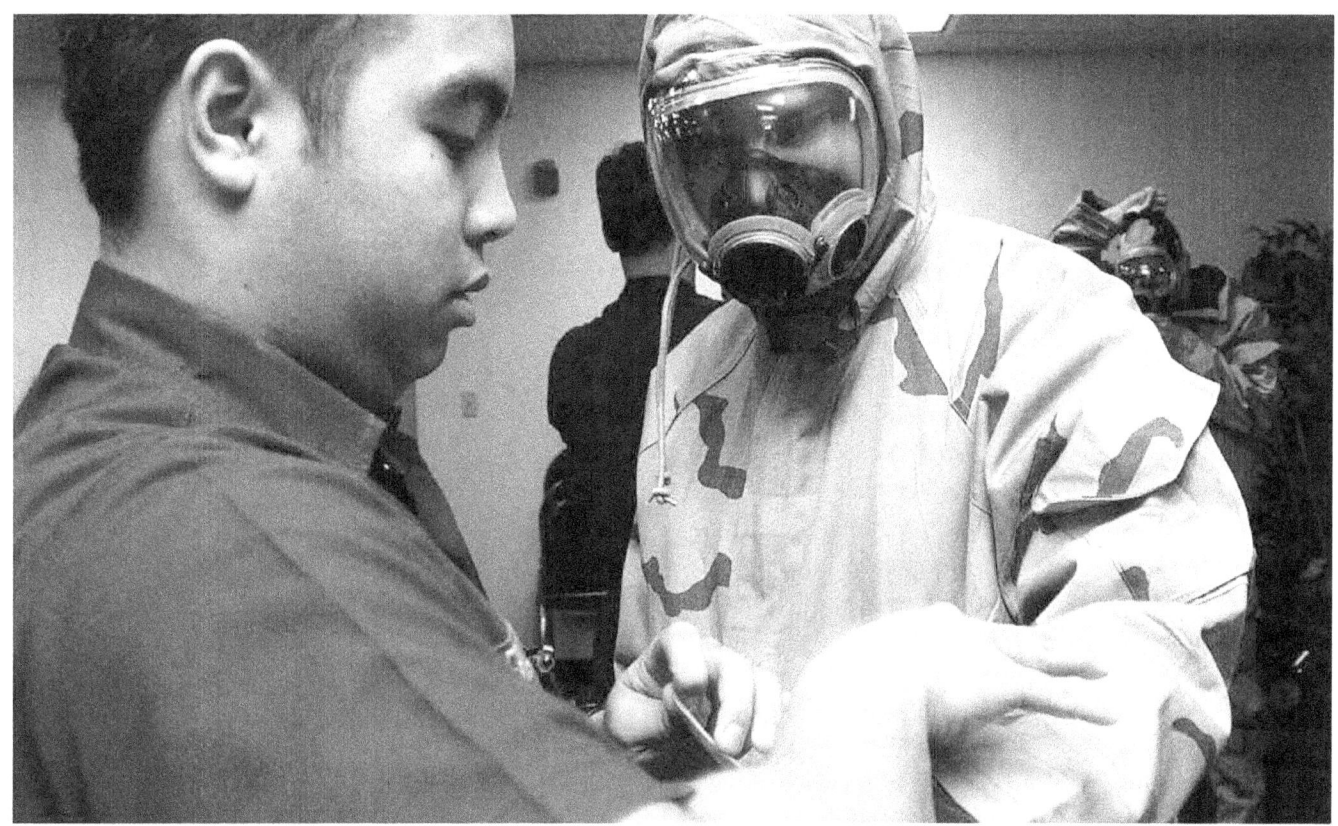

Objective 4.2

Provide scalable and robust all-hazard response capability.

The Nation will know it can rely on us to respond in time of need. We will provide and coordinate a quick and effective response when state, local and tribal resources are overwhelmed by disasters and emergencies. We will bring the right people and resources to bear where and when they are needed most, including medical, urban search and rescue, and incident management capabilities, and will assist all mariners in peril. We will provide integrated logistical support to ensure a rapid and effective response and coordinate among Department of Homeland Security and other federal, state and local operations centers consistent with national incident command protocols. We will work with our partners to create and implement a National Incident Management System and a single, all-discipline National Response Plan that will strengthen the Nation's ability to respond to catastrophic events of all types, including terrorism.

Objective 4.3

Provide search and rescue services to people and property in distress.

Mariners operate in an unforgiving and often remote environment that increases the risk of injury, loss of life and property. We will continue to use our maritime expertise, assets and around-the-clock, on-call readiness to conduct search and rescue missions to save lives and property. We will also continue to partner with other nations, federal, state, local agencies, maritime industry, professional mariners, commercial providers and volunteer organizations to assist mariners in distress and protect property in imminent danger. A number of projects are underway which will improve our ability to respond to maritime distress incidents. Re-capitalization of aviation, surface, command and control architecture and supporting logistic and personnel systems, as well as the procurement of specialized boats and attainment of additional search planning tools will greatly enhance our ability to assist mariners in distress.

For the first time, we will identify and assess threats to the homeland, map those threats against vulnerabilities we see in critical infrastructure, issue warnings to the states and localities and organize protective measures.

- Secretary Tom Ridge

Remarks to the National Association of Counties
March 3, 2003

Recovery

Strategic Goal 5

Lead national, state, local and private sector efforts to restore services and rebuild communities after acts of terrorism, natural disasters, or other emergencies.

Objective 5.1

Strengthen nationwide recovery plans and capabilities.

We will work with our partners to ensure the Nation's capability to recover from multiple or simultaneous disasters, including terrorist use of weapons of mass destruction, other man-made hazards and natural disasters, through the development and maintenance of short- and long-term plans and capabilities.

Objective 5.2

Provide scalable and robust all-hazard recovery assistance.

We will lead the Nation's recovery from the impacts of disasters and emergencies. We will deliver timely and appropriate assistance to individuals and families following acts of terrorism, natural disasters and other emergencies, acknowledging the unique requirements of recovery from catastrophic disasters and weapons of mass destruction events. We will provide help to restore services and public facilities, and provide states and other partners with professional, readily deployable, trained and certified leaders and staff to manage all levels and types of disasters. We will make assistance available to states and local governments for the management, mitigation and control of local hazards and emergencies, which threaten to become major disasters.

Service

Strategic Goal 6

Serve the public effectively by facilitating lawful trade, travel and immigration.

Objective 6.1

Increase understanding of naturalization, and its privileges and responsibilities.

Citizenship through naturalization is the ultimate privilege of the immigration system. We will place renewed emphasis on a national effort to cultivate an awareness and understanding of American civic values and to underwrite commitment to United States citizenship. We will promote education and training on citizenship rights, privileges and responsibilities, to not only enhance the naturalization experience, but also ensure that our immigration system promotes a common civic identity for diverse citizens.

Objective 6.2

Provide efficient and responsive immigration services that respect the dignity and value of individuals.

We will administer immigration laws in an efficient, expeditious, fair and humane manner. To respond to the increased demand for immigration services, we will streamline processes and deploy modern information technology tools to increase the productivity of our employees. We will enhance quality assurance through employee training and monitoring to provide courteous, accurate and responsive service to those who seek and qualify for admission into our country.

Objective 6.3

Support the United States humanitarian commitment with flexible and sound immigration and refugee programs.

The United States has a longstanding tradition of providing protection to individuals who have been persecuted and displaced. Because many applicants for humanitarian program benefits understandably lack documentation, the programs are uniquely vulnerable to abuse. We will combat the risk posed by criminals or terrorists who attempt to exploit these programs, while maintaining our commitment to those who need refuge.

Objective 6.4

Facilitate the efficient movement of legitimate cargo and people.

The border of the future must integrate actions to screen people and goods abroad prior to their arrival in sovereign United States territory to ensure compliance with entry and import regulations. Agreements with our Canadian and Mexican neighbors are central to this effort. America's borders will be made more efficient, posing little or no obstacle to legitimate travel and trade. We will manage our borders to keep pace with expanding trade and migration, while preventing illegal immigrants, illicit drugs and other contraband from entering through the land, air and maritime approaches to our country.

Organizational Excellence

Strategic Goal 7

Value our most important resource, our people. Create a culture that promotes a common identity, innovation, mutual respect, accountability and teamwork to achieve efficiencies, effectiveness and operational synergies.

Objective 7.1

Protect confidentiality and data integrity to ensure privacy and security.

Protecting vital and sensitive information, thus ensuring the privacy of American citizens, is important to the safety of the Nation. We will ensure the technologies employed sustain, and do not erode, privacy protections relating to the collection, use and disclosure of personal information. We will eliminate in appropriate access to confidential data to preserve the privacy of Americans. We will maintain an appropriate balance between freedom and safety consistent with the values of our society.

Objective 7.2

Integrate legacy services within the Department improving efficiency and effectiveness.

We are committed to creating a high-performing, integrated organization. We will collaborate and communicate across legacy agency lines to ensure we have the best most effective mix of services. We expect to optimize mission performance by consolidating and integrating roles and responsibilities; creating better operating processes and procedures; and using the latest technology.

Objective 7.3

Ensure effective recruitment, development, compensation, succession management and leadership of a diverse workforce to provide optimal service at a responsible cost.

We will create a personnel system that is flexible and contemporary while preserving basic civil service principles and merit concepts. We will seek and employ the best and the brightest people our nation has to offer. We will create a cooperative, positive work environment that benefits from the knowledge, experience and active input of employees. We will link individual performance to organizational goals, helping individuals to maximize their potential and contribute fully to the organization.

Objective 7.4

Improve the efficiency and effectiveness of the Department, ensuring taxpayers get value for their tax dollars.

We will maintain continual and unquestionable accountability, responsibility and effective utility of all resources allocated to the Department. We will develop prudent budget requests and evaluate the value received for the expenditures made to ensure the maximum benefit to the country for the tax dollars invested by the American public. With a strong commitment to a streamlined and effective competitive sourcing plan we will create a market-based organization that promotes competition, innovation and choice.

Objective 7.5

Lead and promote E-Government modernization and interoperability initiatives.

The ability to communicate, coordinate and share information is key to ensuring the safety and security of our nation. We will develop productive information sharing relationships within the Department; and with other federal agencies; state, local and tribal governments; international partners; the private sector; and the American public. We will provide appropriate incentives for non-federal entities to increase information sharing with the Federal Government, consistent with privacy and security policies. We will design and implement an information architecture that reflects a national plan for information sharing to optimize interdependencies and strengthen interrelationships. We will use emerging technologies to better manage and disseminate the vital information needed to ensure the safety of American citizens.

Objective 7.6

Fully integrate the strategic planning, budgeting and evaluation processes to maximize performance.

Aligning our activities, core processes and resources to our goals, objectives and resource expenditures is essential. We will rigorously assess, evaluate and measure our performance and appropriately allocate resources to ensure effective stewardship of taxpayer dollars. Our strategic plan provides the foundation for budget development, execution and performance assessment.

Objective 7.7

Provide excellent customer service to support the mission of the Department.

Provide seamless, transparent and dedicated customer support services in the areas of budget, appropriations, expenditure of funds, accounting and finance; procurement; human resources and personnel; information technology systems; facilities, property, equipment and other material resources; and identification and tracking of performance measurements to enable the people in frontline programs to accomplish the mission of the Department effectively.

Dozens of agencies charged with homeland security will now be located within one Cabinet department with the mandate and legal authority to protect our people. America will be better able to respond to any future attacks, to reduce our vulnerability and, most important, prevent the terrorists from taking innocent American lives.

-President George W. Bush

Remarks by the President at the Signing of
H.R. 5005 the Homeland Security Act of 2002

Homeland Security

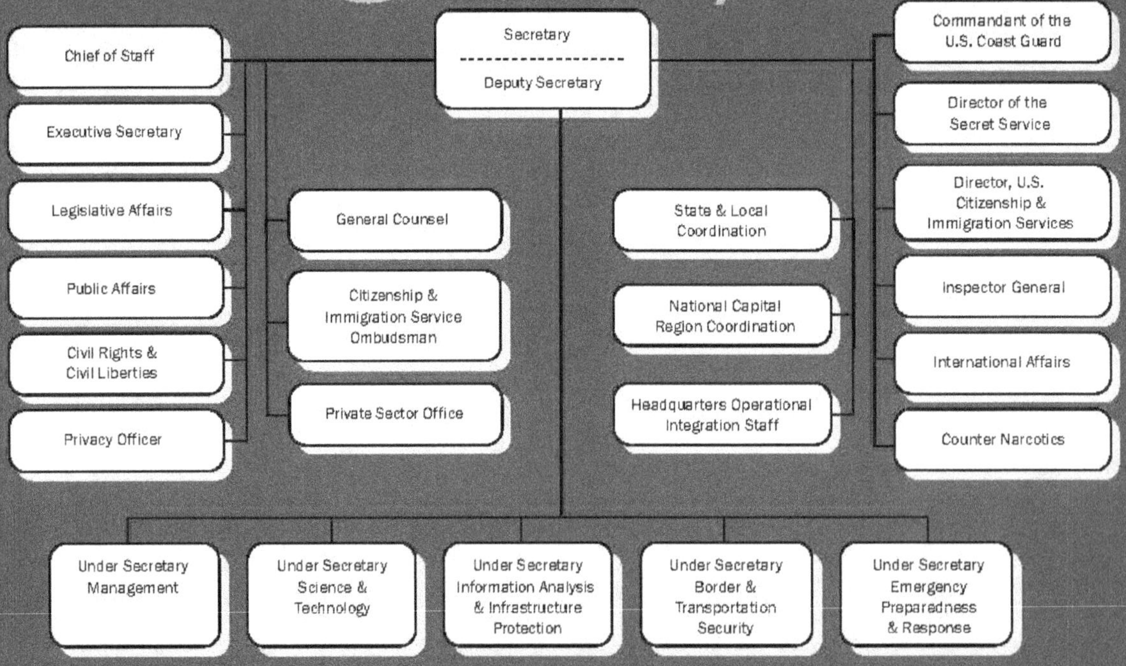

| Chief of Staff |
| Executive Secretary |
| Legislative Affairs |
| Public Affairs |
| Civil Rights & Civil Liberties |
| Privacy Officer |

| Secretary |
| Deputy Secretary |

| General Counsel |
| Citizenship & Immigration Service Ombudsman |
| Private Sector Office |

| State & Local Coordination |
| National Capital Region Coordination |
| Headquarters Operational Integration Staff |

| Commandant of the U.S. Coast Guard |
| Director of the Secret Service |
| Director, U.S. Citizenship & Immigration Services |
| Inspector General |
| International Affairs |
| Counter Narcotics |

| Under Secretary Management |
| Under Secretary Science & Technology |
| Under Secretary Information Analysis & Infrastructure Protection |
| Under Secretary Border & Transportation Security |
| Under Secretary Emergency Preparedness & Response |

A Day in the Life of Homeland Security

The Department of Homeland Security has one mission but uses many tools and areas of expertise to accomplish our goal of securing the homeland. On any given day, we perform a variety of different tasks and functions to make America safer and our citizens more secure. Although our responsibilities are varied, we are united in a common purpose - 24 hours a day, 7 days a week.

Below is a sampling of what the men and women of The Department of Homeland Security do in an average day.

Today, United States Customs and Border Protection agents will:

- Process over 1.1 million passengers arriving into our nation's airports and seaports;
- Inspect over 57,006 trucks and containers, 580 vessels, 2,459 aircraft and 323,622 vehicles coming into this country;
- Execute over 64 arrests;
- Seize 4,639 pounds of narcotics in 118 narcotics seizures;
- Seize an average of $715,652 in currency in 11 seizures;
- Seize an average of $23,083 in arms and ammunition and $467,118 in merchandise;
- Deploy 1200 dog teams to aid inspections;
- Make 5,479 pre-departure seizures of prohibited agricultural items;
- Apprehend 2,617 people crossing illegally into the United States;
- Rescue 3 people illegally crossing the border in dangerous conditions;
- Deploy 350,000 vehicles, 108 aircraft, 118 horses on equestrian patrol and 480 all-terrain vehicles;
- Utilize 238 Remote Video Surveillance Systems, each system using 1-4 cameras to transmit images to a central location; and
- Maintain the integrity of 5,525 miles of border with Canada and 1,989 miles of border with Mexico.

Today, United States Immigration and Customs Enforcement agents will:

- Make 217 arrests on immigration-related violations;
- Make 41 arrests on customs violations;
- Remove 407 criminal aliens and other illegal aliens;
- Investigate 12 cases involving unauthorized employment threatening critical infrastructure;
- Participate in 24 drug seizures resulting in the seizure of 5,511 pounds of marijuana, 774 pounds of cocaine and 16 pounds of heroin;
- Make seven currency seizures, totaling $478,927;
- Make grand jury appearances resulting in the indictment of a combination of 32 people and companies;
- Launch 20 vessels in support of marine operations protecting the territorial seas of Puerto Rico, South Florida, the Gulf of Mexico and Southern California;
- Fly 25 surveillance flights supporting criminal investigations in Puerto Rico and the Continental United States
- Disseminate 80 criminal investigative leads to field offices;
- Review 1,200 classified intelligence cables;
- Protect over 8,000 federal facilities;
- Screen over 1 million federal employees and visitors entering federal facilities;
- Make 6 arrests for criminal offenses on federal property; and
- Intercept 18 weapons from entering federal facilities to include firearms, knives and box cutters.

Today, Transportation Security Agency employees will:

- Screen approximately 1.5 million passengers before they board commercial aircraft;
- Intercept 2 firearms; and
- Deploy thousands of federal air marshals to protect the skies.

Today, the Federal Law Enforcement Training Center will:

- Provide law enforcement training for more than 3,500 federal officers and agents from 75 different federal agencies.

Today, the Office for Domestic Preparedness will:

• Disburse millions of dollars to states and cities across the country.

Today, United States Coast Guard units will:

• Save 10 lives;
• Assist 192 people in distress;
• Protect $2.8 million in property;
• Interdict 14 illegal migrants at sea;
• Conduct 109 search and rescue cases;
• Seize $9.6 million of illegal drugs;
• Respond to 20 oil and hazardous chemical spills;
• Conduct 50 Port Security Patrols;
• Conduct 20 Homeland Security Air Patrols;
• Board 2 high interest vessels;
• Escort 8 vessels, such as cruise ships or high interest ships, in and out of port;
• Embark Sea Marshals on 2 vessels;
• Maintain over 90 security zones around key infrastructure in major ports or coastal areas; and
• Educate 502 people in Boating Safety Courses.

Today the United States Citizenship and Immigration Services will:

• Provide information and services to approximately 225,000 customers in one of its 250 field locations;
• Respond to 75,000 calls to its 1-800 customer service number;
• Naturalize approximately 1,900 new citizens; and
• Process approximately 19,000 applications for a variety of immigration related benefits.

Today, Federal Emergency Management Agency (FEMA) employees will:

- Provide 11,305 fire education publications through FEMA's United States Fire Administration to help Americans better prevent and respond to fires;
- Improve the effectiveness of 220 fire service personnel through courses offered by FEMA's National Fire Academy;
- Help protect 1,000 students at risk for tornadoes by providing their school administrators with information about how to properly construct tornado shelters;
- Provide critical preparedness, prevention, response and recovery information to 2.5 million Americans who access the FEMA website, www.FEMA.gov, each day;
- Provide 4,000 people volunteer opportunities to help better prepare their communities through Citizen Corps at its website, www.citizencorps.gov. The site receives 36,000 hits per day;
- Help save $2.7 million in damages from flooding across the country through the Department's flood plain management;
- Spend $10.6 million to help communities respond and recover from disasters;
- Help protect an additional 104 homes from the devastating effects of flooding through flood insurance policies issued by the National Flood Insurance Program;
- Help 224 Americans recover from disasters by providing direct federal disaster relief assistance in the forms of low-interest loans, unemployment insurance, crisis counseling and temporary housing;
- Partner with the Small Business Administration to provide almost 60 low-interest loans worth approximately $3.6 million to help America's businesses recover from disasters;
- Distribute $45,243 to state and local governments through FEMA's Emergency Management Performance Grants to help develop, maintain and improve their emergency management capabilities;
- Distribute $51,506 through FEMA's Community Emergency Response Team grants to help state emergency managers initiative, organize, train and maintain teams of citizens who are qualified to assist in responding to disasters;
- Provide an average of $917,808 in grants to America's fire departments through the Assistance to Firefighters Grant program;
- Distribute $221,917 through FEMA's Emergency Operations Center grants to state governments to help them develop and improve emergency management facilities; and
- Distribute $218,493 through FEMA's Interoperable Communications Equipment grants to help develop and support communications interoperability among first responders and public safety emergency officials.

Today, Department of Homeland Security Science and Technology employees will:

- Receive approximately 27 new homeland security technology proposals from large and small businesses;
- Receive an average of 6 Homeland Security technology proposals submitted via the science.technology@dhs.gov email address; and
- Meet with an average of 4 industry leaders to discuss new technologies to protect the homeland.

Today, Department of Homeland Security Information Analysis and Infrastructure Protection employees will:

- Receive and review 500 cyber security reports from Internet security firms, government organizations, private companies and foreign governments;
- Review more than a 1,000 pieces of intelligence from the intelligence community and law enforcement agencies; and
- Distribute 4 information bulletins or warning products to critical infrastructure about vulnerability assessments, risk reduction and protective measures.

Today, the United States Secret Service will:

- Protect high profile government officials including the President, the Vice President, visiting heads of state and former Presidents;
- Provide protection to traveling protectees in 17 different cities;
- Screen over 4,000 people entering protective sites;
- Examine 1,500 protective intelligence reports to assess potential threats to protectees;
- Complete 11 protective intelligence investigations to assess potential risk to protectees from individuals or groups;
- Open over 90 new cases involving financial and electronic crime, identity theft, counterfeiting, and personnel security investigations;
- Prevent over $6 million in financial crime losses to the American public; and
- Seize $172,000 in counterfeit currency.

We face a two-pronged challenge; safeguard our homeland, and at the same time, ensure that the free flow of people, goods and commerce is not disrupted. The Department of Homeland Security is leading the effort to reach this objective, but it will not be achieved strictly within the Department of Homeland Security. It will require a sustained and coordinated effort by governmental and private partners. It will require investment by all parties, the development of new approaches and the application of new technologies. It will require us to make difficult decisions, critical assessments and work to find the elusive balance point between the substantial and measurable costs of security and even more substantial and immeasurable costs of insecurity.

-Secretary Tom Ridge

Testimony before the Senate Committee on Commerce, Science and Transportation
April 9, 2003

Key Factors

The Federal Government has a critical role in homeland security, yet the nature of American society and the structure of American governance make it impossible to achieve the goal of a secure homeland through federal executive branch action alone.

The Administration's approach to homeland security is based on the principles of shared responsibility and partnership with the Congress; state, local and tribal governments; the private sector; the American people; and our international partners.

Key factors and assumptions that can significantly affect the achievement of the goals are:

Detection and prevention of terrorist activity.
The prevention of terrorist attacks is the first priority in securing our homeland. Terrorism depends on surprise. With it, a terrorist attack has the potential to do massive damage to an unwitting and unprepared target. Without it, the terrorists are prone to be preempted by authorities and even if they are not, the damage that results from their attacks is likely to be less severe. The United States will take every necessary action to avoid being surprised by another terrorist attack. Achievement of these goals will be influenced by the capabilities of intelligence and warning to detect terrorist activity before it manifests itself in an attack so proper preemptive, preventive and protective action can be taken. Proactive detection of terrorist activities and aggressive prevention of attack will continue. The capabilities of intelligence and warning methods and systems to detect and deter terrorist activity will continue to be strengthened.

Reduction of the threat posed by terrorists.
To reduce the threat posed by terrorists, the United States and our allies must prevent terrorist organizations from obtaining chemical, biological, radiological and nuclear weapons, which pose a threat to our safety and security. The United States and our international partners are committed to denying terrorist organizations the means with which to threaten our citizens. Achievement of these goals will be influenced by the ability of the United States and our allies to disrupt international terrorist organizations, and the ability of federal, state and local governments to interrupt terrorist groups operating within the United States. The efforts of the United States and our international partners will continue to thwart the ability of terrorists to gain expertise in conventional and less traditional means of attack.

Concerted national effort.
The establishment of the Department of Homeland Security involved the most extensive reorganization of the Federal Government in the last fifty years. Achievement of these goals lies in our ability to organize and coordinate the collective efforts of overlapping federal, state and local governments involving more than 87,000 different and sometimes independent jurisdictions plus the private sector and international partners. We will be able to effectively harness the expertise and commitment of state, local and tribal agencies and organizations involved in homeland security, and requisite levels of funding will be provided at the federal, state and local levels and by our international partners. We will collectively develop the shared values and culture necessary to foster interconnecting and complementary work relationships, methods and systems that are reinforcing rather than duplicative to meet our collective requirements for homeland security.

Effective laws.
Throughout our nation's history, we have used laws to promote and safeguard our security and our liberty. Laws at the federal, state and local levels provide mechanisms for the government to act and define the limits of action. Achievement of these goals will be influenced by the enactment of legislation that balances our individual liberties and rights with the safety and security of our nation and our citizens. Appropriate laws will be in place and administered effectively to provide the framework in which we operate and guide our collective efforts to achieve these goals.

Advancements in science and technology.
America's advantage in science and technology is a key to securing our homeland. New technologies will help prevent and minimize the damage from future terrorist attacks. Just as science helped us defeat past enemies overseas, it will also help us defeat the efforts of terrorists to attack our homeland and disrupt our way of life. Achievement of these goals will be influenced by the application of advancements in science and technology to mitigate the risks posed by modern terrorism. Investment in revolutionary capabilities with high payoff potential will yield solutions that can be fielded to enhance our safety and security.

International cooperation.
In a world where terrorists do not respect traditional boundaries, our strategy for homeland security cannot stop at our borders. The collective efforts of America and our international partners will influence our achieving these goals. America will pursue a sustained, steadfast and systematic international agenda to counter the global terrorist threat and improve our homeland security. The intense international anti-terrorism campaign will continue. The ability of the United States to prevent potential terrorists from attacking our homeland depends on the sustained commitment of the American people and the international community to defeating terrorism wherever it appears.

Implementation

To ensure the safety of our nation, we will provide capabilities of public value, build capacities on a national scale and secure domestic and international support. This strategic plan is the foundation for our efforts. We are establishing an overarching framework for implementation of this plan as part of our *Future Years Homeland Security Plan*. This framework integrates strategy, organizational structure, operations and culture with the formulation of our budget. Although we have made substantial progress, important work remains.

Our priorities to implement this plan are:

Address mission fragmentation and overlap.
As the first step to optimize the convergence of 22 disparate agencies into the new department, we are reviewing existing activities and organizational structures. As part of our program assessment and evaluation process, we will identify fragmentation, overlap and omission. We will design and implement organizational structures to optimize discrete mission areas, and establish frameworks for intradepartmental coordination among crosscutting interdependent efforts. We will ensure performance measures used are complementary and mutually reinforcing.

Risk Management.
We will guide our actions with sound risk-management principles that take a global perspective and are forward-looking. Risks must be well understood, and risk management approaches developed, before solutions can be implemented. Many of the Department's actions are already guided by a risk management approach to some extent, and the evolution towards a more comprehensive picture of risk and threat will facilitate better performance measurement. Managing risk is a continuous process that requires constant vigilance. As part of managing risk, we assess continuously what can go wrong; evaluate the potential consequences if an event happens, determine the likelihood of an attempt succeeding, prioritize the risks; and implement strategies to deal with those risks. We will direct our resources toward those priority threats and vulnerabilities based on potential consequences and likelihood of a success.

Establish a results-oriented organizational culture.
We will give our employees and partners a clear sense of the results we want to achieve to maximize performance, affect accountability and foster sound decision-making. We will accomplish this through investments of time and resources, sustained focus and consistent demonstration of the unwavering commitment by our leaders to achieve results. We will provide decision-making authority commensurate with assignment of responsibility for achieving our goals. We will recognize and reward our employees and partners for helping accomplish our objectives.

Develop meaningful, outcome-oriented performance goals and collect useful performance data.
We will monitor and report accomplishments as they relate to progress toward achieving our strategic goals. Over the next year we will align all programs in the budget to specific objectives supporting the Department's strategic goals. We will establish, beginning in the FY06 budget request, performance measures for each program to measure our success in achieving the supported objective. We will review the level and type of activities, products and services delivered and the results of those efforts to examine the extent to which objectives are being achieved. We will balance the competing goals of collecting information needed to assess performance with giving agencies or states and localities the flexibility needed to effectively implement the Department's programs.

Use performance information in allocating resources.
This strategic plan is the cornerstone of the *Future Years Homeland Security Plan,* which will be the roadmap for the Department. Our budget request will be structured to implement this strategic plan. We will link planned performance with budget formulation in a simplified and streamlined manner to ensure the budget requests in our *Future Years Homeland Security Plan* are directly aligned to achieve these strategic goals. We will report our progress annually, and consult with Congress, the Administration and other key stakeholders to reassess and evolve our mission and long-term goals, as well as the strategies and resources they require.

Evaluation

As a newly formed department, we are in a period of profound transition. We are establishing a foundation of national policies and initiatives that will further secure our homeland in the face of evolving external trends that include diverse security threats and increasing global interdependence. While we face an array of challenges, we have an unprecedented opportunity to restructure the operation of the Federal Government to address the needs of our society and enhance collective performance.

During this unique time of convergence, it is vital that we examine and carefully assess homeland security programs and activities to ensure that they are appropriate and effective.

To this end, we established a program evaluation and analysis division under our Chief Financial Officer to create an 'evaluation culture' throughout the Department. We are undertaking a fundamental review of our programs and subordinate organizations to bring about synergy and clarity. This is a task of immense proportion. It is not easy. Nonetheless, we have a unique opportunity to institute 21st century management principles to ensure that the Department has the characteristics and capabilities needed to effectively leverage people, processes and technology to achieve the results our citizens deserve.

Our approach is to:

Integrate strategy and execution.
Considering agencies that are now a part of the newly formed department have their own priorities, interests and citizen service base, we are creating a unifying culture that fosters commitment to self-examination. We are developing a *Future Years Homeland Security Plan* that will translate our strategic goals into specific programs and allocate the resources required to achieve results. We will institute measures of effectiveness throughout the Department that center around critical behaviors and outcome-related performance to focus our daily activities on fulfilling our objectives.

Assess performance, evaluate results and report progress.
We will assess, through objective measurement and systematic analysis, the manner and extent in which our programs achieve these goals. Through the Department's assessment and evaluation process we will compare our performance to the expectations established by the *President's Management Agenda*. Using the Office of Management and Budget's Program Assessment Rating Tool, we will evaluate the purpose, design and execution of our focus areas and major efforts to determine their overall effectiveness. We will establish measures of effectiveness to assist in establishing future strategies and prioritizing resources, and, if needed, we will develop performance improvement and corrective action plans. Our annual Performance and Accountability Report to the Administration and Congress will contain an evaluation of our progress towards achieving goals.

Collaborate.
We will engage in meaningful dialogue with stakeholders regarding our progress in implementing the *National Strategy for Homeland Security*. We will consult with the Homeland Security Advisory Council; Congress; other federal departments; and our state, local, tribal and international partners to review continuing trends and address emerging issues. Given resource constraints in the context of other national needs, collaboration will enhance decision making between the Congress and the Executive Branch regarding the appropriate mix of long-term strategies needed to address the challenges our nation faces.

Refine.
Through continuous program assessment and evaluation we will identify gaps that are formed by developing issues and changing circumstances. We will refine performance goals based on measures of effectiveness. We will continuously evaluate results-oriented performance information as a routine part of decision making, at all levels, to address evolving trends and emerging threats. To remain agile and enhance daily performance, we will reorient our direction as conditions warrant, immediately or more deliberately.

Communication

The *National Strategy for Homeland Security* is the foundation of this strategic plan. It was the product of more than eight months of intense consultation across the United States. The Administration talked to thousands of people – from governors and mayors, state legislators and members of Congress to concerned citizens and foreign leaders. This strategic plan brings our collective vision of the future into focus, and articulates the Nation's commitment to secure the homeland and protect our citizens. We will sustain the same levels of intense participation and inclusive consultation during implementation of this plan. Together, we will leverage our collective talents to create a secure homeland through a partnership based on mutual trust and cooperation.

Through credible and effective communication with our stakeholders, we will seek to understand and then address the important issues and priorities that face us. With testimony, reports, briefings and information sessions, we will inform members of Congress and their staffs of our progress in accomplishing these goals and objectives. We will apprise the American people of the security status of our homeland, and conduct outreach campaigns through the media to educate our citizens regarding what they can do to help keep America safe and secure. With the understanding that it is often the unknown that leads to fear, we will inform the public of potential threats as warranted, and help our citizens better prepare for and react to natural and man-made disasters when they do occur.

We will communicate this plan to the American people and our employees using a variety of complementary means. In the belief that a well-informed workforce will ensure a cohesive effort to defend the homeland, we will launch this plan with a series of Internet-based educational sessions for our employees. Publicized through our intranet, these sessions will include video remarks by the Secretary and feature personal discussions by key leaders. Companion printed products will be distributed to our workforce; state, local and tribal organizations; private sector and international partners. With the knowledge that public awareness will heighten the Nation's alertness, we will make this plan and an accompanying video available on the Internet. A printed version will be available to the public upon request.